The Unexplained

Kate Jaeger

OXFORD
UNIVERSITY PRESS

is a department of the University of Oxford.
It furthers the University's objective of excellence in research, scholarship,
and education by publishing worldwide in

Oxford   New York
Auckland   Cape Town   Dar es Salaam   Hong Kong   Karachi
Kuala Lumpur   Madrid   Melbourne   Mexico City   Nairobi
New Delhi   Shanghai   Taipei   Toronto

With offices in

Argentina   Austria   Brazil   Chile   Czech Republic   France   Greece
Guatemala   Hungary   Italy   Japan   Poland   Portugal   Singapore
South Korea   Switzerland   Thailand   Turkey   Ukraine   Vietnam

Oxford is a registered trade mark of Oxford University Press
in the UK and in certain other countries

Text © Kate Jaeger 2007

The moral rights of the author have been asserted

Database right Oxford University Press (maker)

First published 2007

British Library Cataloguing in Publication Data

Data available

ISBN: 978-0-19-846123-4

7 9 10 8

Printed in China

Paper used in the production of this book is a natural,
recyclable product made from wood grown in sustainable forests.
The manufacturing process conforms to the environmental
regulations of the country of origin

Acknowledgements

The publisher would like to thank the following for permission to reproduce photographs: **p4/5**bgrnd
The Hubble Heritage Team (STScI/AURA)/NASA; **p5**l Corbis UK Ltd., **p5**r Sygma/Corbis UK Ltd.;
p7 Luc Novovitch/Alamy; **p8** Mary Evans Picture Library/Alamy; **p10** Evening Standard/Getty Images;
p11t Hartmut Schwarzbach/Argus/Still Pictures, **p11**b John Cutten/Mary Evans Picture Library;
p12 Bernard Gotfryd/Getty Images; **p13**t Michael Powell/Rex Features, **p13**b UPP/TopFoto; **p14** Prakash
Singh/AFP/Getty Images; **p15** Bazuki Muhammad/Reuters/Corbis UK Ltd.; **p16** Bettmann/Corbis UK Ltd.;
p17t Andreas Manolis/Reuters/Corbis UK Ltd., **p17**b Mary Evans Picture Library/Alamy; **p18** Roy Jennings/
Frank Lane Picture Agency; **p19** Mary Evans Picture Library/Alamy; **p20** Bob Krist/Corbis UK Ltd.;
p21 Chris Knapton/Alamy; **p22**t Kevin Schafer/Alamy, **p22**b Yann Arthus-Bertrand/Corbis UK Ltd.;
p23 Yann Arthus-Bertrand/Corbis UK Ltd.

Cover: Corbis

Illustrations by Hemesh Alles: **p21**; Mark Duffin: **p16**; **p20**, **p22**; Andy Parker; **p9**

Contents

The world can be a mysterious place! Sometimes things that seem extraordinary or impossible can be explained, but others cannot – despite all our modern scientific knowledge. In this book read about:

- extraordinary places and events
- the theories offering possible explanations.

Amazing aliens	4
Unidentified flying objects	6
Kidnapped by aliens!	8
Superhuman powers	10
Uri Geller	12
How do they do that?	14
Extraordinary events	16
The Bermuda Triangle	16
Great balls of fire	18
Places of mystery	20
The world's most remote home	20
Drawings in the desert	22
Glossary and Quiz	24

Amazing aliens

Every year, thousands of people claim to have seen aliens or their spaceships. Is it possible that life could exist elsewhere in the universe? Could **extraterrestrials** be visiting our world, capturing human beings, or even living amongst us here on Earth?

Many people think it is unlikely that our planet is the only place in the universe where life exists. Scientists are trying to find some proof for the existence of life in outer space.

Is there anybody out there?

Since 1960, a project known as the *Search for Extra-Terrestrial Intelligence* (SETI) has used huge radio telescopes to scan the universe for radio messages sent by distant life forms. If aliens are sending radio messages, SETI has not yet heard them, or found any proof that intelligent life exists in space.

Life on Mars?

In 1984, a **meteorite** from Mars containing tiny pieces of **fossilised** living matter was discovered in Antarctica. This very exciting discovery seems to be the first real proof that there could have been life on Mars.

A magnified picture of fossilised living matter found in a Mars meteorite.

Unidentified flying objects

Have you ever seen strange lights or flying objects
in the sky and wondered what they are? Whilst most
unidentified flying objects (UFOs) can easily be explained,
others remain a mystery. Could they be spaceships bringing
alien visitors from far away across the universe?

The Roswell Incident

One of the most famous UFO sightings happened in Roswell,
New Mexico, USA in 1947. William 'Mac' Brazel saw an
explosion during a thunderstorm and went to investigate. On
the ground he found some thin but incredibly strong pieces
of metal; some pieces were decorated with strange symbols.
Mac reported what he had found to the nearby
Air Force base.

The Air Force announced that they had found a 'Flying Saucer', but later said that they had a made a mistake and the metal had come from a crashed **weather balloon**. Was the Air Force trying to cover something up?

If this was a spaceship from another world, who was flying it? According to some witnesses four small grey aliens with big heads were found at the crash site. Some nurses working at Roswell Air Base Hospital said the aliens were brought there to be examined. In 1996, a film showing the aliens was released, but this turned out to be a **hoax**.

Kidnapped by aliens!

There are many reports of encounters with visitors from outer space. Some people even claim to have been taken aboard their spaceships!

An alien encounter...

One night in 1957, a Brazilian farmer, Antonio Villas Boas, saw a strange flying object in the sky. The next day he claims to have been dragged on board an egg-shaped spaceship by three aliens. They covered him in a clear liquid and took some of his blood. After Antonio's release, doctors examined him and found marks and scars which he said had been caused by fighting with the aliens. He suffered from sickness and sleepiness as if he had been poisoned. Do you think Antonio's story is true or do you think there might be another explanation?

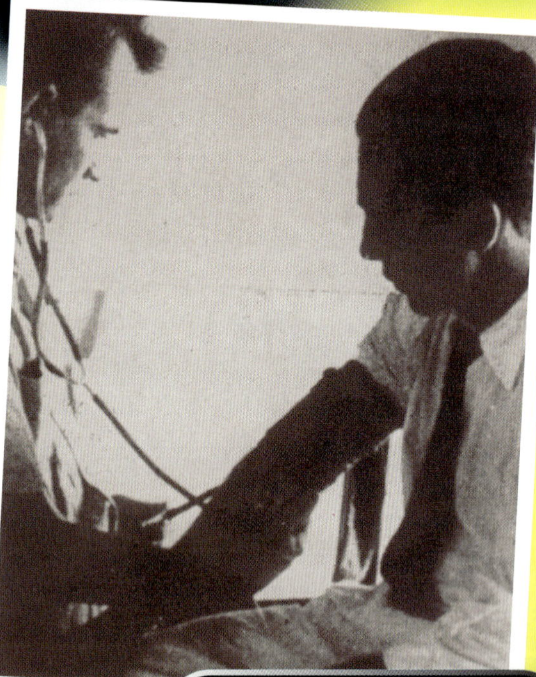

Antonio Villas Boas being examined by a doctor after claiming to have been captured by aliens

So what might aliens look like? These are some types of alien that people claim to have seen:

- Greys – small, grey-skinned, human-like creatures with big pear-shaped heads and huge eyes.

- Men in Black – aliens dressed in black suits and ties with very pale skin. These aliens visit people who have seen UFOs and warn them not to talk about it.

- Nordics – tall aliens with yellow hair and blue eyes.

Superhuman powers

It's not only superheroes who claim to have special powers! There is evidence that some people have mysterious **psychic powers** that cannot be explained. Here are some examples:

Telepathy

If you were lucky enough to be telepathic you could receive and send information just by thinking about it. Imagine if you could talk to someone else without speaking; it would be great for secret conversations. It is often members of the same family, especially twins, who claim they can communicate in this way.

The Ball brothers, both of whom are Anglican **bishops**, and identical twins, claim to have experienced instances of telepathy.

Dowsing

This is the ability to find water, metals, precious stones, and hidden objects with the help of metal or wooden sticks held above the ground. Some people who have this power use it to help mining companies find hidden natural resources such as oil or diamonds.

Searching for water with a 'dowsing rod' on the African savanna.

Psychokinesis

Also known as telekinesis, this is the power to change things in the world around us using the mind. Moving an object around, or stopping a watch, just by thinking about it, are examples of psychokinesis.

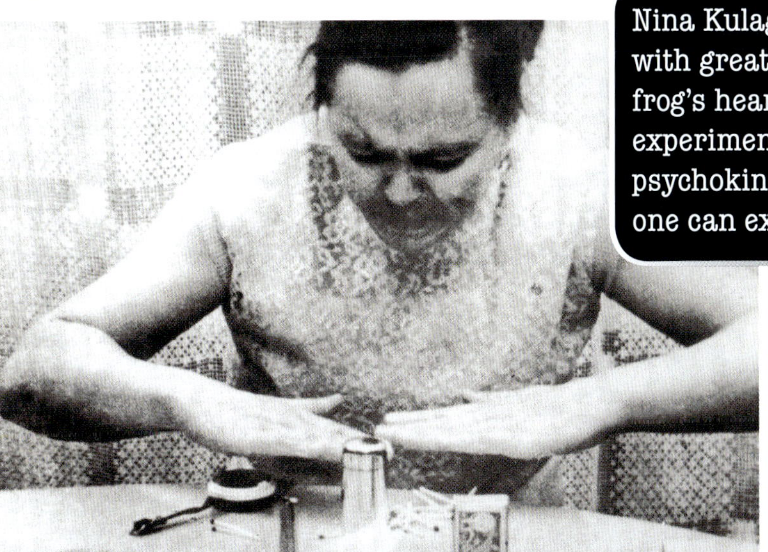

Nina Kulagina, a Russian woman with great powers, was able to stop a frog's heart beating in a laboratory experiment set up to investigate her psychokinetic powers in 1970. No one can explain how she did this.

Uri Geller

Born in 1946 in Israel, Uri Geller is famous for his mind-bending psychic powers. He first noticed his special powers at the age of five when a spoon crumpled in his hand and broke. He later became famous, especially for his ability to bend spoons and other metal objects.

Here are just some examples of the things he claims to have achieved using the power of his mind:

- 1975 – during an experiment at the Stanford Research Institute in the USA, Uri Geller correctly guessed eight out of ten throws of a dice. The chances of doing this are a million to one.
- 1984 – he erased all the information from a computer in Tokyo in the presence of scientists.
- 1989 – he stopped London's **Big Ben** for three hours.

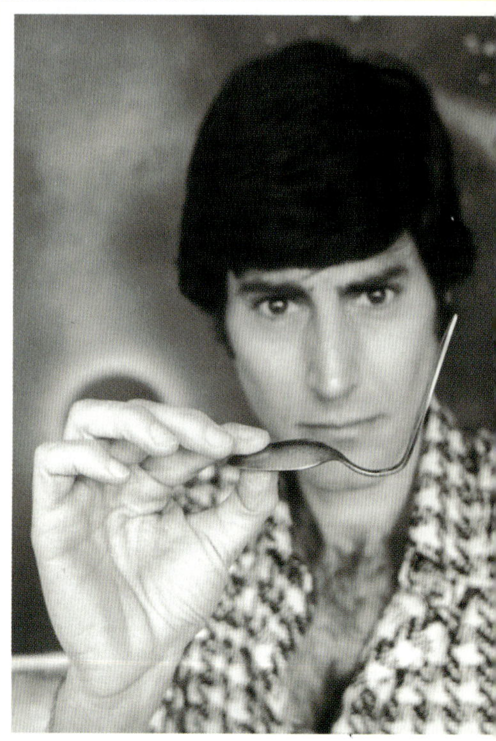

Does Uri Geller really have superhuman powers, or is it all a hoax? Many scientists have carried out experiments on him to try to answer this question. As a result of their experiments some scientists have decided that it is possible that Uri Geller has special psychic powers.

Uri Geller's 1976 Cadillac is covered with over 5000 pieces of bent cutlery, that he bent with the power of his mind.

Lying on a bed of nails or walking on burning coals might seem painfully impossible! But human beings can carry out amazing challenges that would make even the strongest and bravest superhero proud. How do they do it? Do they have superhuman powers?

Lying on nails

You might think that lying on a bed of sharp nails would be very uncomfortable, but in fact people can do this without injuring themselves at all. Because the weight of the person is spread evenly across all the nails, the nails do not break the skin. No superhuman powers needed here!

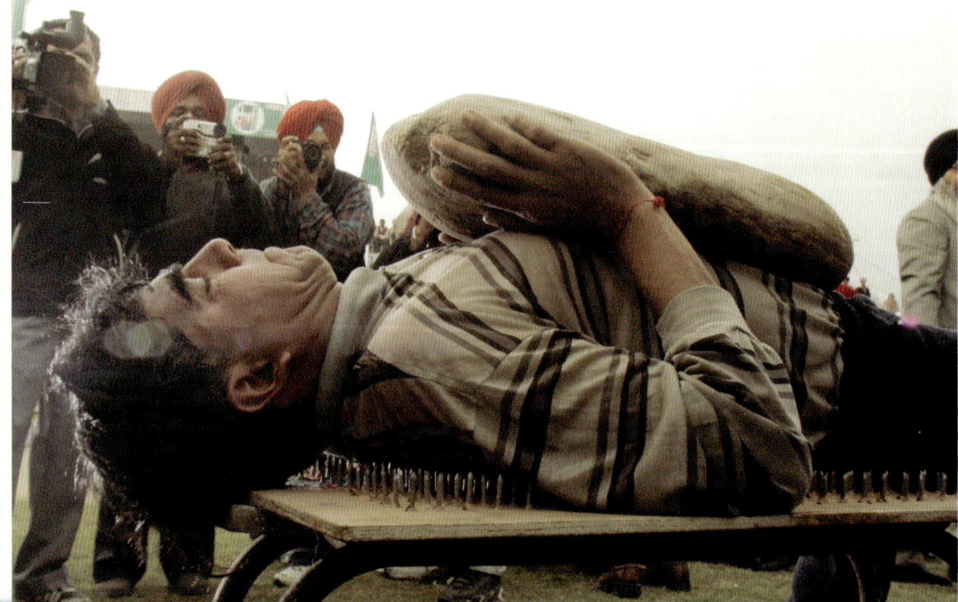

Walking on fire

In many parts of the world, walking on burning wood or hot coals is part of a **religious** ritual. The holy men who perform this feat do so without getting burnt or experiencing any pain. Can the power of the mind overcome the pain? Do these men have special powers? Or is there another explanation?

The secret is in the kind of fuel used for the fire and the amount of time it has been burning. Some types of wood, for example, do not get especially hot when they burn, and it is these that are used for fire walking. The fire is then left to burn for some time. This allows a layer of ash to form over the top of the fire which protects anyone walking on it. The final secret is to remember to walk very quickly!

Extraordinary events

Science can often help to explain strange happenings but some extraordinary events will probably always remain a mystery.

The Bermuda Triangle

Many ships and aeroplanes have disappeared without trace whilst passing through the area known as the Bermuda Triangle. Could there be strange forces at work?

Inside the Bermuda Triangle:
- air pilots have reported seeing strange lights following their planes
- compasses give strange readings, and radios and radars stop working
- the sea has been seen to bubble and froth.

The US Navy ship *Cyclops*, along with its crew of 300 men, vanished without a trace in 1918.

The Bermuda Triangle is defined by imaginary lines linking Bermuda, Puerto Rico, and Florida.

Sudden violent storms, strong currents, and underwater earthquakes can explain many of the disappearances. But what about the strange lights, compass readings, and bubbling seas? Explanations include:

- ball lightning (see pages 18 and 19)
- unusual magnetic fields – which might cause compasses to behave oddly so that ships could get lost
- trapped gases released from rocks beneath the ocean. Scientists think that these gases not only make the sea bubble, but can build up around a ship, making it sink suddenly into the ocean depths.

More extrordinary events...

The famous 'ghost' ship the *Marie Celeste* was found drifting off the coast of Portugal in 1872. The ship was deserted and there was no trace of the ten people on board.

Great balls of fire

Ball lightning remains one of science's great unsolved mysteries. Despite eye witness accounts going back to the Middle Ages, and decades of scientific investigation, we still don't know what it is.

Ball lightning is different from flash lightning we see during thunderstorms.

- It appears as glowing balls of light that can last for several seconds.
- It can hover and move slowly in the air, or roll and bounce along the ground before quickly disappearing or exploding into flames and sparks.
- Although it is usually between the size of a golf ball and a football, in 1987 two park rangers in Australia reported seeing ball lightning 100 metres across.
- Anything in its path is destroyed and set on fire. It can even kill people. So if you see it, remember not to stand in its way!

There are many theories about what ball lightning is. Could it be UFOs from outer space, or even fairies and spirits? Scientists think that ball lightning is actually caused by **electrically charged particles** – but we don't know how or why it happens.

More extraordinary events...

Could electrical charges also explain the bizarre event of spontaneous human combustion? This is when a person suddenly bursts into flames – for no reason. Strangely, the things around them do not catch fire.

Places of mystery

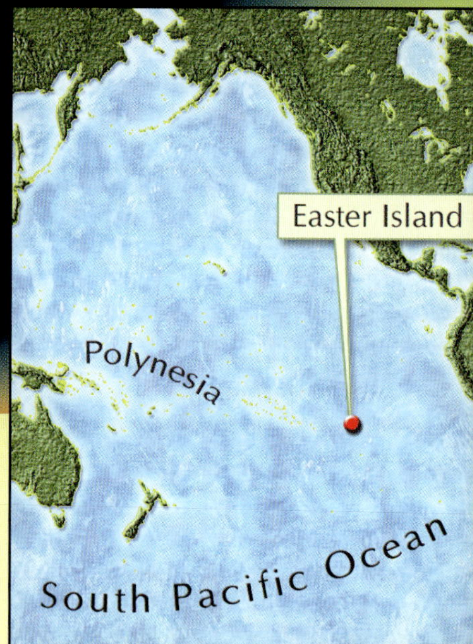

Ancient sites around the world are often places of mystery. Sometimes there are things that are difficult to explain, such as why and how they were built and who built them.

The world's most remote home

Easter Island in the South Pacific Ocean is one of the most remote islands in the world – 2000 kilometres from the nearest land. You might think there would be no one living at such a remote place, but people have lived there for 1500 years.

Ancient stone statues, called *moai*, are found throughout Easter Island and these give us a clue about how people came to be living there.

The Easter Island statues were made between 500 and 1000 years ago and vary in size from two to nine metres. There are around 800 of these statues on the island, and it is thought they represent important chiefs and gods.

Similar statues are found on many of the islands in **Polynesia**. It is thought that people travelled 3500 kilometres from Polynesia to Easter Island in wooden canoes. It is amazing that they ever found Easter Island in the middle of the vast ocean.

The people of Polynesia were skilled **seafarers** able to travel hundreds of miles in canoes like this.

More mysterious places...

Stonehenge in Wiltshire, England is one of the world's best known ancient stone circles. It was built over 4000 years ago, but no one knows exactly how or why. One interesting feature is that the sun's rays shine straight into the middle of the stone circle on midsummer's morning (21st June).

Drawings in the desert

The Nazca Desert in Peru, South America, is home to some of the world's most amazing and mysterious structures made by humans: the Nazca lines. Made 1400–2200 years ago, they can only be seen clearly from the air.

Monkeys, spiders, lizards, and hummingbirds are some of the animals that stare up from the desert floor.

The largest design is a huge bird with a zigzag neck and long beak. It is over 300 metres long.

Geometric shapes include wedges with sides up to 800 metres long and straight lines that stretch for up to 3 kilometres.

How were the lines made?

They were made by moving the rocks and pebbles that cover the surface of the desert to reveal the lighter coloured earth below. Because the Nazca desert is one of the driest places on earth – it only rains for 20 minutes a year – the lines have been preserved for over 2000 years.

What were they for?

There have been suggestions that the Nazca lines are landing strips for alien spacecraft! It is not known why these drawings were made, but people living in the area today believe that they were made for religious reasons to thank the gods for the water that flows into the region from the Andes mountains. Without this water people would not have been able to live in the dry Nazca desert.

More mysterious places...

The writings of the ancient Greek **philosopher** Plato tell of the rich and powerful island of Atlantis which once ruled over parts of Europe and Africa, but sank one day beneath the waves without trace. Did Atlantis really exist, where was it, and how did it vanish overnight?

Glossary

Big Ben – the name given to the famous clock at the Palace of Westminster in London

bishop – a high-ranking Christian priest in charge of a particular area

electrically charged particles – small pieces of matter which are charged with electricity making them attract each other

extraterrestrial – a living being from another planet

fossilised – when a plant or animal that has been in the ground for a very long time becomes hardened within the rock around it

hoax – a trick used to fool people about something which is not true

meteorite – the remains of a piece of rock or metal from space that falls to Earth

philosopher – someone who studies ways of thinking about life and human behaviour

Polynesia – a large group of over 1000 islands in the Pacific Ocean

psychic powers – the ability to perform special feats using the power of the mind

religious – to do with people's beliefs in a god or gods

seafarer – someone who travels at sea

weather balloon – a balloon containing equipment which sends information back to Earth about weather conditions

Quiz

Can you find the answers to these questions in this book?

1. In 1984, a meteorite containing fossilised living matter was found in Antarctica. Which planet did it come from?

2. What are the chances of correctly guessing eight out of ten throws of a dice?

3. Where did the US navy ship *Cyclops* disappear in 1918?

4. Name one difference between ball lightning and the lightning we usually see during thunderstorms.

5. On which date each year do the sun's rays shine straight through the middle of Stonehenge?